Open Earth: Mammals Unlocked
Hardcover first edition • November 2023 • ISBN: 978-1-958629-29-1
eBook first edition • November 2023 • ISBN: 978-1-958629-14-7

Written by Dia L. Michels, Text © 2023
Illustrations by Bonnie Hofkin, Illustrations © 2023

Project Manager, Cover and Book Design: Caitlin Burnham, Washington, D.C.
Senior Editor: Sarah Cox, Bremerton, WA
Editors:
  Marlee Brooks, Chevy Chase, MD
  Hannah Thelen, Silver Spring, MD
Editorial Assistants:
  Jennifer Coon, Shannon Dinniman, Carmina López, Claire Romine, Charlotte Shao, Susan Stark

Coming soon in paperback and bilingual English/Spanish.
  Bilingual English/Spanish Paperback first edition • May 2024 • ISBN: 978-1-958629-15-4
  Spanish eBook first edition • May 2024 • ISBN: 978-1-958629-16-1
  English Paperback first edition • November 2024 • ISBN: 978-1-958629-13-0

Teacher's Guide available at the Educational Resources page of ScienceNaturally.com.

Published by:
  Science, Naturally! – An imprint of Platypus Media, LLC
  750 First Street NE, Suite 700
  Washington, DC 20002
  202-465-4798 • Fax: 202-558-2132
  Info@ScienceNaturally.com • ScienceNaturally.com

Distributed to the book trade by:
  National Book Network (North America)
    301-459-3366 • Toll-free: 800-462-6420
  CustomerCare@NBNbooks.com •NBNbooks.com
  NBN International (worldwide)
    NBNi.Cservs@IngramContent.com • Distribution.NBNi.co.uk

Library of Congress Control Number: 2023940934

10 9 8 7 6 5 4 3 2 1

Printed in China.

OPEN 🔑 EARTH

MAMMALS

UNLOCKED

Written by Dia L. Michels

Illustrations by Bonnie Hofkin

Science, Naturally!
An imprint of Platypus Media, LLC
Washington, D.C.

Dear Reader,

On a daily basis, you probably interact with more mammals than you realize. You may cuddle up with a mammal at bedtime, but scream when you see one in the hallway in the middle of the night. You may feed one at the zoo and then eat one for dinner. You may hear one scurrying about in your basement or flying around in your attic. Our relationship with mammals can get complicated. We love them, we live with them, we fear them.

Mammals Unlocked is my third book about this unique class of animals. My interest in mammals was sparked during my first pregnancy. Instead of a joyous mother-to-be basking in her pregnancy glow, I was a wreck. For me, it was a nightmare of endless morning sickness, fatigue, and panic attacks. I seriously wondered whether I was carrying a child or a monster!

Nine months on the sofa gave me a lot of time to think about mammalian motherhood. Fast forward three decades and I am still thinking about it. What can we learn from seeing how different species reproduce and raise their offspring? Is our goal for maturity to be independent or interdependent? How do we learn the skills we need for survival?

All mammals share three key features (as you will learn in the first chapter!). And yet, among the thousands of mammal species, there are so many differences. Some count their time on this planet in months; others live for centuries. Some rarely leave their tree branch; others roam thousands of miles every year. Some live happily munching on leaves; others must hunt to survive.

There is no quick way to study mammals. You could spend your whole life learning about just one species. But the more we learn about these fascinating creatures, the more we learn about ourselves. Who doesn't watch fondly as a mother elephant nurtures her newborn, or laugh at a chimpanzee's playful antics? And who doesn't reel in horror when a winded elk is overtaken by a snarling wolf pack?

You are about to embark on an exciting exploration of mammals and their habitats—from blistering deserts to icy glaciers, from tangled rainforests to wide open plains, from mountain heights to ocean depths. I hope this book unlocks for you the world of mammals and leaves you standing in awe of these amazing creatures.

From one mammal enthusiast to another… happy reading!

—Dia

For the humans, cats, and dogs who
bring me such joy!
-D.L.M.

To Bill. My anchor. My confidant.
My best friend. Maaaah!
-B.H.

For my parents, who instilled in me
a love of learning.
-S.C.

Acknowledgments

Writing this book was quite an undertaking. Though I earned the author credit, it was a team effort that involved months of research, endless fact-checking, and hours of discussion. We discovered mammals we had never heard of before and learned new facts about common ones. Every answered question opened up a dozen new questions, leading us back to further research and discussion. I am grateful to my amazing team: Caitlin Burnham, Sarah Cox, Ellen Roberts, Claire Romine, Marlee Brooks, and Hannah Thelen.

Table of Contents

Chapter 1

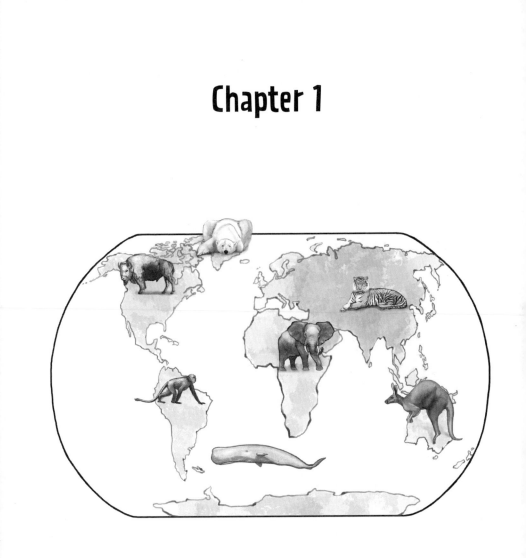

The Wonderful World of Mammals

The Wonderful World of Mammals

The world of mammals is filled with thousands of amazing species. Mammals come in all sizes, from the tiny, squeaking mouse to the huge, trumpeting elephant. Some mammals have coats of thick fur, others have armor-like skin, and some even have scales. Mammals live all over the world and in all types of habitats. There are mammals in the desert, in the forest, in the city, in the ocean, up in the sky, and under the ground. Though mammals may look very different from each other, they all have the same key features that distinguish them from other animals. Read on to discover the wonderful world of mammals!

Question 1

True or false?
All mammals are animals.

Question 1
True or false? All mammals are animals.

Domain	Eukarya
Kingdom	Animalia
Phylum	Chordata
Class	Mammalia
Order	Pilosa
Family	Megalonychidae
Genus	Choloepus
Species	Two-Toed Sloth

Answer: True

Living organisms, from plants to people, are divided into the following categories: domain, kingdom, phylum, class, order, family, genus, and species. An easy way to remember this is "<u>D</u>aring <u>K</u>ing <u>P</u>hillip <u>C</u>ame <u>O</u>ver <u>F</u>rom <u>G</u>erman <u>S</u>hores." All animals are in kingdom Animalia. All mammals are in class Mammalia. Thus, all mammals are animals because they are part of kingdom Animalia. So, all mammals are animals, but not all animals are mammals. Some animals may be in a different class, such as Reptilia or Amphibia.

Question 2

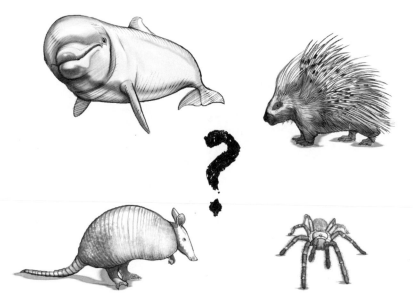

Which of the following animals is not a mammal?

a) Armadillo
b) Tarantula
c) Dolphin
d) Porcupine

13

Question 2
Which of the following animals is not a mammal?

Answer: b) Tarantula

Three key features are found exclusively in mammals: hair or fur, three middle ear bones, and females who produce **milk** to feed their babies. No other class of animals has these three features. Even though a tarantula looks furry, its "hairs" are not true hair. A tarantula has no mammalian features; it belongs to a completely different class: Arachnids. Tough-skinned armadillos, slippery dolphins, and prickly porcupines do not appear furry like most other mammals, but they each have some form of hair, as well as the other two mammalian features.

True or false?
Humans are mammals.

Question 3
True or false? Humans are mammals.

DOMAIN	Eukarya
KINGDOM	Animalia
PHYLUM	Chordata
CLASS	Mammalia
ORDER	Primate
FAMILY	Hominidae
GENUS	Homo
SPECIES	Homo sapiens

A Mammal with "CLASS"

Answer: True

Humans are biologically classified as mammals. We are our own species of mammal called *Homo sapiens*, which means "wise man" in Latin. There are many differences that separate us from the rest of the mammal world. For example, we wear clothes, we cook our food, and we can write. But we are classified as mammals because we have the same three special features of mammals: we have hair, we have three middle ear bones, and our mothers produce milk to feed us when we are babies.

Question 4

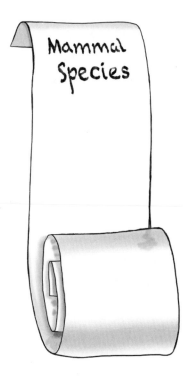

Mammal
Species

How many different species of mammals are there?

17

Question 4

How many different species of mammals are there?

Answer: Over 6,400

A species is the most specific category of **classification** for living organisms. Mammals within a species are very similar and are able to breed with each other. There are over 6,400 different species of mammals in the world and more are discovered each year. Some types of mammals have very few species, while others have many. For example, there is only one known species of platypus, but there are almost 1,000 different species of bats. Mammals live all over the world—on all seven continents and in all five oceans.

When two mammals from different species reproduce, what is their young called?

a) Subspecies
b) Hybrid
c) Taxon
d) Bi-breed

Question 5
When two mammals from different species reproduce, what is their young called?

Answer: b) Hybrid

Sometimes two different species are purposely bred because the resulting **hybrid** has better qualities than either parent. The mule, which is the product of a male donkey and a female horse, has been bred since ancient times because it is strong and sure-footed. Hybrids may also occur in the wild when the **habitats** of two different species overlap. Polar bears and grizzly bears in the Canadian Arctic have been known to interbreed, producing a hybrid called a pizzly or grolar bear. Hybrids are not their own species, as they are generally unable to produce babies.

Question 6

Though some mammals have fins to swim or wings to fly, most mammals move around on four _____.

Question 6

Though some mammals have fins to swim or wings to fly, most mammals move around on four _____ .

Answer: limbs

Kangaroos jump, elephants shuffle, monkeys swing, armadillos waddle. The world of mammals has many different forms of movement. All land mammals have two sets of jointed body parts, called **limbs**, with which they move their bodies. For mammals who move on all fours, such as elephants and armadillos, their limbs are referred to as front legs and hind legs. For mammals who move in an upright position, such as kangaroos and monkeys, their limbs are called arms and legs.

Question 7

True or false?
If a mammal is a predator, its eyes are
set in the front of its head.

Question 7
True or false? If a mammal is a predator, its eyes are set in the front of its head.

Answer: True

Predatory mammals, such as cats, weasels, and bears, hunt other animals for food. Their eyes are set in the front of their heads, allowing them to see depth and distance when they chase their prey. Mammals such as deer, rabbits, and goats are preyed upon by other animals. **Prey** mammals have eyes that are set on the sides of their heads, allowing them to see predators approaching from the side. Some prey mammals, such as sheep, can even see behind themselves without turning their heads.

Which of the following terms describes a mammal that eats both meat and plants?

a) Binovore
b) Polyvore
c) Macrovore
d) Omnivore

Question 8
Which of the following terms describes a mammal that eats both meat and plants?

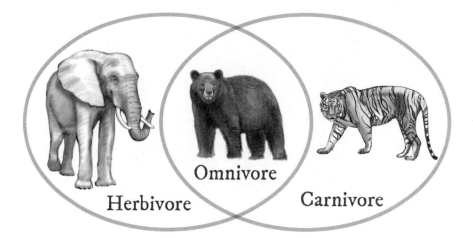

Omnivore

Herbivore

Carnivore

Answer: d) Omnivore

Mammals can be categorized by what type of food they eat. Bears are **omnivores** because they eat a wide variety of foods, including berries, nuts, insects, fish, and other mammals. Plant-eaters such as elephants are called **herbivores**. Cats hunt animals for meat, so they are called **carnivores**. Anteaters are called **insectivores** because they mostly eat ants and other insects. Orangutans primarily eat fruit, so they are called **frugivores**. Vampire bats are **sanguivores**, which means they feed on blood.

A mammal with a(n) _____ tail is able to use it for holding onto objects such as tree branches or pieces of food.

27

Question 9

A mammal with a(n) _____ tail is able to use it for holding on to objects such as tree branches or pieces of food.

Answer: prehensile

Prehensile comes from a Latin word that means "to grasp." A prehensile tail has highly developed muscles and acts like a fifth limb, able to wrap around branches, hold onto objects, and even support the mammal's body weight while hanging upside down. For example, a spider monkey might wrap its tail around a tree branch to anchor itself and then reach downward to pick a piece of fruit from another branch. Other mammals with prehensile tails include opossums, tree porcupines, and binturongs.

Question 10

True or false?
All mammals can make sounds
to communicate.

Question 10
True or false? All mammals can make sounds to communicate.

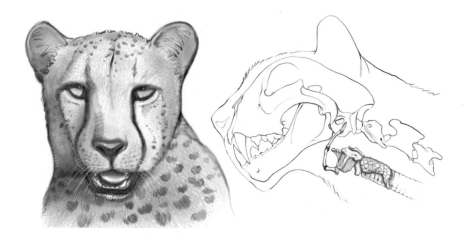

Answer: True

Lions roar, cows moo, mice squeak, dolphins click, cheetahs purr, hippos grunt, hyenas laugh, giraffes hum—all mammals have a special part of their throat, called the **larynx**, that allows them to make sounds to communicate. Mammals make different noises depending on the situation. For example, a dog might bark if it is happy, whimper if it is scared, or whine if it is lonely. A vervet monkey can make different warning sounds depending on if a predator is a leopard, an eagle, or a snake. Mammals also make specific sounds for protecting their territories, attracting mates, and identifying their young.

Ungulates are mammals that have
_____ instead of paws.

Question 11

Ungulates are mammals that have _____ instead of paws.

Answer: hooves

Ungulates get their name from the Latin word *ungula*, which means "hoof." Instead of paws, these mammals walk around on hooves, which are basically giant toenails. Most large land mammals are ungulates, and are divided into two groups: odd-toed and even-toed. Odd-toed ungulates include horses, tapirs, and rhinos. Even-toed ungulates, such as deer, pigs, camels, and cows, have two toes covered by hooves, which looks like a single hoof split in half. These ungulates are also referred to as "cloven-hoofed."

Chapter 2

On the Farm

On the Farm

Mammals such as horses, cows, sheep, and pigs have lived and worked alongside humans for thousands of years. Farm mammals play an important role in human life all over the world. Depending on the species, these mammals may be used for transportation or field work. They may be ridden or used to pull carts. They help graze land, and their waste even fertilizes the soil. Others may be raised for **milk**, meat, **wool**, or leather. Even though they live mostly outdoors, farm mammals are tame rather than wild. But being tame does not mean these mammals are boring. Off to the farm!

The process for teaching a mammal to depend on humans for food and shelter is called

_____.

Question 12

The process for teaching a mammal to depend on humans for food and shelter is called _____ .

Answer: domestication

A **domesticated** mammal is a species that has been tamed to meet people's needs, such as transportation, protection, clothing, and food. Most farm mammals, like horses, cows, sheep, and pigs, have been domestic for thousands of years. This is also true for mammals that are kept as pets, such as dogs and cats. It is possible to find wild species that are related to domestic mammals; for example, the Mongolian wild horse or the coyote. A truly domesticated species depends on human care and would not easily survive in the wild.

Question 13

How long does a cow chew its food?

Question 13
How long does a cow chew its food?

Answer: For about eight hours

When a cow takes a mouthful of food such as grass or hay, it does not chew it completely before swallowing. This is because a special part of the cow's stomach, called the **rumen**, will actually send the partially-chewed plant material, or cud, back into the cow's mouth to be chewed more. This process, called "chewing the cud," takes about eight hours until the tough, fibrous plant material is broken down enough for the cow to digest it. A cow is referred to as a **ruminant** because of how it eats and digests. Other ruminant mammals include sheep, goats, deer, and giraffes.

What is the standard way to determine a horse's age?

a) Length of tail
b) Size of hooves
c) Condition of teeth
d) Color of muzzle

Question 14
What is the standard way to determine a horse's age?

Answer: c) Condition of teeth

A horse's teeth change throughout its lifetime. Horses are born toothless, and the first teeth they grow, called "milk teeth," eventually fall out. By the time a horse is about five years old, it will have all of its permanent teeth. Horses are not ruminants, so they must chew their food completely before swallowing. Hours of rhythmic chewing movements throughout a horse's lifetime create specific patterns of wear on its teeth. For example, a young horse has wide, flat teeth, but an older horse's teeth have been worn down to a more triangular shape.

Question 15

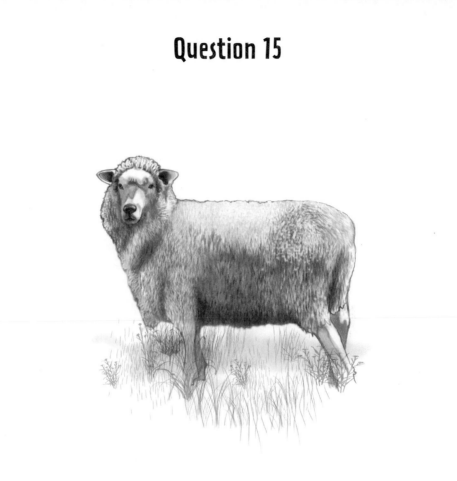

A sheep's fine, curly hair is called _____.

Question 15

A sheep's fine, curly hair is called _____ .

Answer: wool

Have you ever wondered how a sheep's wool becomes a piece of clothing? First, the sheep is sheared, which is just like getting a haircut. This is done in the spring to help the sheep stay cool in the summer. Then the clipped-off coat, called a **fleece**, is sorted to separate the rough fibers from the soft ones. The wool is then cleaned to remove oil, dirt, and hay. Next comes carding, where the wool is combed through metal teeth to smooth and straighten it. Finally, it is spun into yarn, which can be woven to make fabric or knitted to make garments.

How many times a day does a mouse eat?

Question 16
How many times a day does a mouse eat?

Answer: 15 to 20 times

Despite its small body and tiny stomach, a mouse eats as often as it can. This is usually 15 to 20 times a day, depending on how much food it can find. Because a mouse uses up so much energy as it scurries around, it must eat often. A mouse will eat just about anything, but prefers grains, fruits, and seeds. During the summer when a mouse can find many things to eat, it saves some food for winter by storing it in places like empty burrows, under rocks, or even in the nooks and crannies of old houses.

Question 17

A llama is related to which of the following mammals?

a) Horse
b) Camel
c) Deer
d) Goat

Question 17
A llama is related to which of the following mammals?

Answer: b) Camel

Native to South America, the llama is part of the camel family. An adult llama is about the size of a large pony, with skinny legs and a long neck, but it does not have a humped back like a camel. In South American countries, llamas have been used for thousands of years for transportation, work, clothing, and food. Llamas have become popular farm mammals because their hair can be spun like sheep's wool to make textiles. Llamas also have a strong guarding instinct and are often used to protect livestock.

Question 18

The _____ is a species of cattle known for its humped shoulders.

Question 18

The _____ is a species of cattle known for its humped shoulders.

Answer: zebu

Native to southern Asia, the zebu is a small breed of cow with some uncommon features: droopy ears, horns that point upward, and a saggy neckline called a **dewlap**. But the zebu's defining feature is the large hump on top of its shoulders. Made of muscle and fat cells, the hump contains lots of blood vessels that release heat through the skin, which helps the zebu stay cool. This is important because the zebu lives in very hot climates. Many native peoples in Africa and Asia use zebus for transportation and farm work, dairy, meat, and leather.

Question 19

True or false?
Donkeys are stubborn and unintelligent.

Question 19
True or false? Donkeys are stubborn and unintelligent.

Answer: False

A member of the horse family, the donkey has been used for thousands of years for work and transportation. Though donkeys are usually portrayed as stubborn and unintelligent, they are actually very smart mammals. Studies have shown that donkeys have a great memory and can remember complicated routes. While some mammals run away if they are threatened, a donkey will assess the situation and decide whether to fight back or run for safety. This is why a donkey might seem stubborn and unintelligent, when in fact it is taking time to make a decision.

Question 20

How many different colors can a dog see?

Question 20
How many different colors can a dog see?

Answer: Three

It was long thought that dogs could only see different shades of gray. However, scientists have since learned that dogs are also able to see blue and yellow, though the colors do not look as bright as they do for humans. Dogs are color blind to red and green, meaning that these colors are hard to tell apart. For example, if a dog seems to ignore a red toy on green grass, it is most likely because the toy is hard to see. But if the toy is yellow or blue, the dog will be able to see it better and want to play.

Question 21

True or false?
A cat is able to land on its feet if it falls.

Question 21
True or false? A cat is able to land on its feet if it falls.

Answer: True

A cat's body is lightweight and flexible, allowing it to jump up to or down from heights of about eight feet. As graceful as a cat usually is, sometimes it may get spooked or distracted and fall from a significant height. If this happens, its body is specially designed to twist in mid-air so that the cat falls on all fours instead of on its back, usually saving it from injuries. This is called the "righting reflex," since it allows the cat to land right-side up. The saying, "a cat has nine lives," came from this remarkable ability to survive falls.

Question 22

Which of these farm mammals is commonly raced for entertainment?

a) Pig
b) Lamb
c) Cow
d) Goat

Question 22
Which of these farm mammals is commonly raced for entertainment?

Answer: a) Pig

Pig races are a popular form of entertainment in countries such as the United States and the United Kingdom. This family-friendly pastime is usually found at state fairs, celebrations, and charity events. Young pigs are small and quick, and love to run for short distances. The miniature racetrack may include easy obstacles such as tunnels, gates, or ramps. Each pig wears a little vest that is either numbered or color-coded. The winning pig is given a tasty treat, such as a cookie, for its prize.

Chapter 3

Through the Jungle

Through the Jungle

Jungle comes from the Hindi word *jangal*, which describes a tropical forest that has dense vegetation from the ground up. A rainforest is like a jungle, but the trees are so tall that they block out most of the Sun, preventing other plants from growing on the forest floor. These tropical forests can be found in regions around the equator, such as Africa, South America, and Asia. Though jungles and rainforests occupy a very small percentage of the Earth's surface, they are home to half of all plant and animal species. Find out about the fascinating mammals that live in this wet and wild **habitat**.

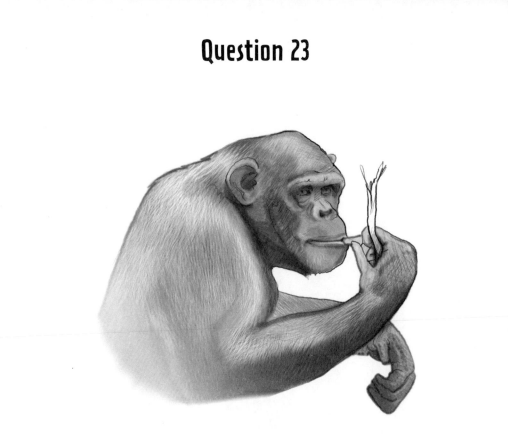

What is the most visible difference between an ape and a monkey?

a) Ears
b) Tail
c) Nose
d) Fur

Question 23

What is the most visible difference between an ape and a monkey?

Answer: b) Tail

The terms "ape" and "monkey" are often confused. Though apes and monkeys are both **primates**, they are each in their own category. The easiest way to tell the difference between an ape and a monkey is the tail: an ape does not have a tail, but a monkey does. Another noticeable difference is body shape and structure. Ape species, such as chimpanzees, have a more upright form and larger shoulders to support their weight while swinging from tree branches. Monkey species, such as langurs, have a more lean, cat-like form and use their tails to help them move through trees.

A tiger is called a(n) _____ predator because it is not hunted by other animals for food.

Question 24

A tiger is called a(n) _____ predator because it is not hunted by other animals for food.

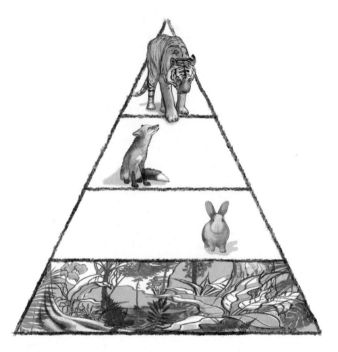

Answer: apex

The word *apex* means the very top of something; in this case, a **food chain**. A food chain is the order in which living organisms depend on each other for food. For example, a rabbit eats grass, a fox eats the rabbit, and a tiger eats the fox. Both the fox and the tiger are **predators,** but since the tiger is at the very top of the food chain, it is known as an **apex predator**. A tiger hunts other animals for food, but no other animal—whether mammal, reptile, or bird—hunts a tiger for food.

Question 25

How long is a giant anteater's tongue?

Question 25
How long is a giant anteater's tongue?

Answer: About 24 in, which is about 60 cm

A giant anteater's tongue is about as long as a child's shoelace. It is pink and shaped like a piece of spaghetti. Giant anteaters are **insectivores**, eating mostly ants and termites. The giant anteater uses its long, sticky tongue to reach inside an anthill or termite mound and slurp up as many insects as possible. Since it has no teeth, it must swallow its food whole. A giant anteater can flick its tongue in and out of its mouth 150 times per minute, which allows it to consume up to 30,000 ants and termites each day.

True or false?
The "river wolf" is the largest wolf in
the Amazon rainforest.

Question 26

True or false? The "river wolf" is the largest wolf in the Amazon rainforest.

Answer: False

There are no wolves in the Amazon rainforest. The "river wolf" is properly known as the giant otter. As the longest member of the weasel family, an adult giant otter can span the length of a twin-size bed. The giant otter makes its home along the Amazon river in South America. It is called the "river wolf" because, like a wolf, it is at the top of the food chain in its habitat. A fast swimmer with sharp teeth and strong jaws, the giant otter is an expert hunter. It eats mostly fish and other **aquatic** animals, such as turtles, frogs, and even snakes.

Question 27

The saola is a shy, hoofed mammal that is related to which of these?

a) Pig
b) Koala
c) Hippo
d) Cow

Question 27
The saola is a shy, hoofed mammal that is related to which of these?

Answer: d) Cow

Native to Vietnam and Laos, the saola (pronounced SOW-la) is in the cow family, though it looks more like an antelope. The saola has a dark brown coat and white facial markings. Both the male and female saola have a pair of long, close-set horns which, from a distance, look like one single horn. This is one reason why the saola is nicknamed the "Asian unicorn," but also because it is so rarely seen. In fact, scientists did not even know the saola existed until about 30 years ago. Since then, it has been photographed in the wild only a few times.

Question 28

How small is a Kitti's hog-nosed bat?

Question 28
How small is Kitti's hog-nosed bat?

Answer: About the size of a quarter

The world's smallest mammal is Kitti's hog-nosed bat. As the name implies, its nose resembles a pig's snout. An adult bat's body is just a little larger than a quarter. Its wingspan is about the same as that of a small songbird. Also known as the bumblebee bat because of its tiny size, the hog-nosed bat can live for as long as 10 years. It is native to parts of Thailand and Myanmar, making its home in limestone caves or outcroppings along rivers, where it eats small, flying insects. Like most bat species, the hog-nosed bat lives in groups, called **colonies**.

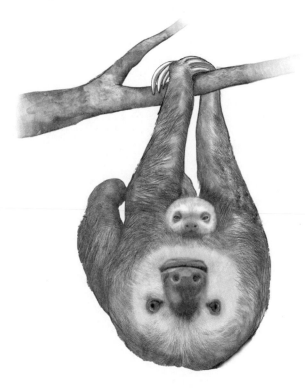

True or false?
A sloth's fur looks green.

Question 29
True or false? A sloth's fur looks green.

Answer: True

The sloth is the world's slowest-moving mammal. It hangs upside-down in the trees and spends most of its day sleeping. Because it lives in the humid rainforest and moves so slowly, a sloth's fur actually starts to grow algae on it, which turns its brown fur a light green color. Algae is a tiny water plant, which you often see floating on the surface of a pond. Though it seems strange that a plant would grow on fur, this is helpful to the sloth because its green fur can act as **camouflage**, allowing the sloth to blend in with the trees.

Question 30

Which of the following jungle mammals has the loudest call?

a) Howler monkey
b) Leopard
c) Bush dog
d) Gorilla

Question 30
Which of the following jungle mammals has the loudest call?

Answer: a) Howler monkey

One of the noisiest mammals in the world, the howler monkey communicates with tremendously loud calls, which sound like deep growls. Its call is so loud that it is about the same noise level as a jet engine at takeoff. Howler monkeys live in the treetops and are very **territorial**, which means they are extremely protective of their area of the jungle. Each morning and evening, groups of howler monkeys make their growling calls back and forth to each other as a warning to stay out of their territory.

Question 31

A tapir's trunk-like snout is called a(n) _____ .

Question 31

A tapir's trunk-like snout is called a(n) _____ .

Answer: proboscis

The word *proboscis* comes from a Greek word that means "to feed." This special kind of snout is very unusual in the mammal world. A tapir's proboscis combines its nose and upper lip, and is actually a special organ for smelling and grabbing food. Just like an elephant's proboscis, or **trunk**, a tapir has a **prehensile** proboscis with which it can grab plant material and put it in its mouth to eat. A tapir spends a lot of time in the water, so it can also use its proboscis like a snorkel while swimming.

How much does the world's largest rodent, a capybara, weigh?

Question 32
How much does the world's largest rodent, a capybara, weigh?

Answer: About 150 lbs, which is about 68 kg

Even though a capybara weighs as much as a very large dog, it is actually in the same family as mice and rats. The capybara lives all over South America in marshy areas along streams or rivers, where it eats grass and water plants. A **semi-aquatic** mammal, the capybara spends a lot of time in the water. It has webbed feet and is an excellent swimmer. If it sees a predator, it can hide underwater for as long as five minutes. The capybara is a very social mammal, and other, smaller animals will often hitch a ride on a capybara's back.

True or false?
Jungle habitats are home to many feline
species, but no canine species.

Question 33

True or false? Jungle habitats are home to many feline species, but no canine species.

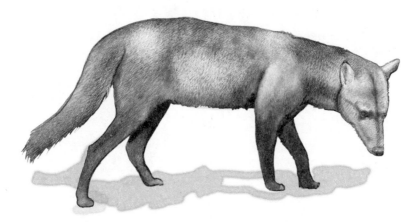

Answer: False

Big cats such as tigers and jaguars are often associated with jungle habitats, but some **canine** species live there too. The short-eared dog is found deep in the Amazon rainforest of South America. It is the only canine species **endemic** to the Amazon, meaning that it lives nowhere else in the world. The short-eared dog is named for its small, bear-like ears. It has a slender body, a bushy tail, and webbed feet for swimming in rivers. Unlike most canines that live in **packs**, the short-eared dog is a **solitary mammal**. It is so rarely seen that some people call it a "ghost dog."

Chapter 4

Over the Mountains

Over the Mountains

Though many different mammal species live in the mountains, they each have unique features that allow them to survive the rugged habitat. North American mountain goats have special hooves designed for climbing on rocky surfaces. Chinchillas have thick fur that keeps them warm high up in the Andes mountains. Tibetan yaks have large lungs that allow them to get enough oxygen at high altitudes. Mountain mammals live at many different elevations, from the base to the top. Some live in trees, some live in rocky crevices, and some even live on sheer cliff faces. Lace up your hiking boots and get ready to encounter some majestic mountain mammals!

True or false?
A moose will avoid the water
because it cannot swim.

Question 34
True or false? A moose will avoid the water because it cannot swim.

Answer: False

The moose is the largest member of family Cervidae, which includes deer and elk. An adult male moose is about the size of a Clydesdale horse, and has huge, shovel-shaped antlers. Even though a moose has a large, bulky body, it can actually swim very well. A moose will swim in lakes or rivers to cool off during the summer or escape from **predators**. It can even dive to the bottom to graze on underwater plants. The moose's nostrils close shut when it dives so that water does not go up its nose.

The marmot, a type of large ground squirrel, spends the winter in _____ , safe and warm in its burrow.

Question 35

The marmot, a type of large ground squirrel, spends the winter in _____ , safe and warm in its burrow.

Answer: hibernation

In places where food is scarce during the long, cold winter, some mammals go into a extended period of inactivity in order to survive. This is called **hibernation**. Marmots begin their hibernation in early fall. While some mammals, such as bears, hibernate by themselves, 10–20 marmots hibernate as a group, or **colony**. Then, in late spring, the colony comes out of the burrow and spends the summer eating, raising their babies, and soaking up the warm sunshine. Marmots eat so much during the summer that they become fat; this extra fat helps them survive the harsh winter.

Question 36

Which of the following is <u>not</u> a name for the mountain lion?

a) Panther
b) Cougar
c) Puma
d) Lynx

Question 36

Which of the following is <u>not</u> a name for the mountain lion?

Answer: d) Lynx

The mountain lion is known by many different names, including panther, cougar, and puma. A mountain lion does not roar like a true lion, but instead makes sounds more like a house cat: hissing, purring, and screaming. In proportion to its body size, the mountain lion has the largest hind legs of any cat, or **feline**, species, giving it the ability to leap great distances and run extremely fast. Native to North and South America, mountain lions can be found wherever there are deer, which are their primary food source. The mountain lion has no natural predators.

Question 37

How often does a buck lose its antlers?

Question 37
How often does a buck lose its antlers?

Answer: Once a year

A male deer, called a buck, loses its antlers once a year, usually between mid-winter and mid-spring. It does not hurt the buck when it loses, or casts, its antlers. The antlers that fall off are called **shed antlers**, and are often used in home decorating or carved into beautiful knife handles. Over the summer, the buck will grow a new set of antlers. By the time breeding season arrives in the fall, it will have a fully grown set of antlers with which to attract female deer and fight off other bucks.

True or false?
Beavers choose a new mate each
breeding season.

Question 38
True or false? Beavers choose a new mate each breeding season.

Answer: False

Unlike some mammals that choose a different mate each year, beavers mate for life. Once a beaver chooses a mate, it stays with that mate for as long as they are both alive. If a beaver's mate dies, it might choose a new one. Each year, a mother beaver gives birth to a **litter** of about six babies, called kits. Both mother and father beaver are active in caring for and training their kits. They live together as a family unit for about two years until the kits are old enough to leave and find their own mates.

The wolverine is called a(n) _____
because it often eats the leftover meat
from another mammal's prey.

Question 39

The wolverine is called a(n) _____ because it often eats the leftover meat from another mammal's prey.

Answer: scavenger

The largest member of the weasel family, the wolverine looks like a small bear with a skunk-like body and very large paws that help it walk on top of snow. Even though a wolverine is able to hunt, it often just eats the leftovers from another **carnivore's** kill. This habit is called **scavenging**. If a wolverine has had enough to eat at one time, it will bury the leftovers to eat later. The wolverine has a strong sense of smell and can find where it hid the leftovers, even buried deep in the snow.

Question 40

How big is a gray wolf?

Question 40
How big is a gray wolf?

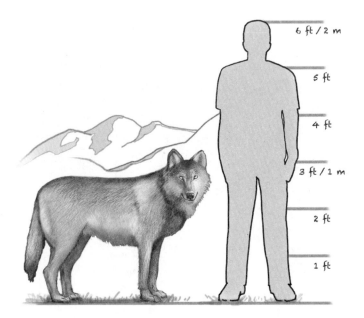

6 ft / 2 m
5 ft
4 ft
3 ft / 1 m
2 ft
1 ft

Answer: Nearly 3 ft, or 1 m, tall at the shoulder

The gray wolf is the largest of all **canine** species. If a gray wolf were standing next to an average-height man, the gray wolf's head would be at the same level as the man's waist. The gray wolf can be found in North America, Europe, and Asia, living in groups called **packs**, which average about six members. A wolf pack usually includes sibling wolves of different ages, headed up by the father and mother wolf. The gray wolf is best known for its howl, which is how it communicates with other gray wolves.

Question 41

True or false?
Black bears are always black.

97

Question 41
True or false? Black bears are always black.

Answer: False

The American black bear's coat can also be brown, cinnamon, or even blond. It is thought the name "black bear" came from sightings by early settlers, since most bears in this species are indeed black. The color of a black bear's coat often depends on which region of North America it lives in. Black bears that live in shady, wooded areas, such as East Coast forests, usually have a dark coat. Black bears that live in western states, near open plains, often have a lighter colored coat, which keeps them from overheating in areas with no shade.

The Himalayan tahr is considered a(n) _____ species because it causes problems in regions outside its natural habitat.

Question 42

The Himalayan tahr is considered a(n) _____ species because it causes problems in regions outside its natural habitat.

Answer: invasive

The Himalayan tahr is a type of goat, native to the Himalayan mountains of Asia. It was introduced to regions in North and South America, New Zealand, and South Africa, but has since become an **invasive species** because of its negative impact on non-native habitats. The Himalayan tahr threatens many plant species by either eating too many or trampling them, which then causes soil erosion. In an effort to help control the Himalayan tahr population in its non-native habitats, some countries allow regulated hunting of the species.

Question 43

Pikas, members of the rabbit family, are known to share their burrows with which of these animals?

a) Snakes
b) Squirrels
c) Toads
d) Birds

Question 43

Pikas, members of the rabbit family, are known to share their burrows with which of these animals?

Answer: d) Birds

Pikas look like round, fluffy rabbits with little ears and short legs. They live in cold **habitats** high up in the mountains, where they nest in rock crevices. During the summer, pikas collect edible plants with which they build their nest for the winter. Instead of hibernating, pikas survive the cold weather by eating the dried plants in their nest. This "haypile" also makes a good winter home for little birds called snowfinches. Their body heat adds extra warmth to the nest, which benefits both the pikas and the snowfinches. This type of close relationship between two different kinds of animals is called **symbiosis**.

Question 44

True or false?
Bighorn sheep live high up in the
mountains but are not good at walking
on rocky surfaces.

Question 44

True or false? Bighorn sheep live high up in the mountains but are not good at walking on rocky surfaces.

Answer: False

Bighorn sheep are master mountain-climbers, able to leap from rock to rock and walk safely on cliff edges. They have split hooves that work like clothespins, pinching onto rocks and ledges. The spongy middle of each hoof helps bighorn sheep keep their footing, while the protective outer hoof is hard enough to dig into snow or ice. Native to the western mountain ranges of North America, bighorn sheep are named for the massive set of curled horns that the males grow. Females also grow a set of horns, though they are much smaller and only slightly curved.

Chapter 5

In the Bush

In the Bush

Though "the bush" is usually associated with Australia, the African bush is equally as notable. Bush **habitats** are vast, undeveloped areas of wilderness that have never been cleared or farmed. Depending on geographic location, bush habitats look very different from each other, such as the eucalyptus forests of Australia compared to the grassy scrubland of Africa. Few people live in bush areas because of the remote conditions, but many species of mammals thrive there. Bouncing bandicoots, flying foxes, and wallowing warthogs are just a few of the many bush mammals. Head to the backcountry for a closer look at wilderness wildlife.

Question 45

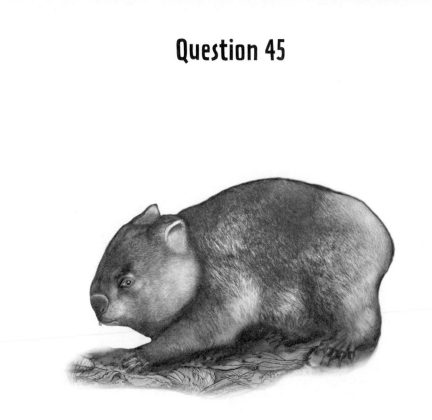

What is the wombat's main defense?

a) Teeth
b) Claws
c) Legs
d) Rump

Question 45
What is the wombat's main defense?

Answer: d) Rump

Native to Australia, the wombat is a **marsupial**, meaning that it carries its babies in a pouch. The wombat has a bear-like body and is about as big as a medium-size dog. Though a wombat can bite, scratch, and run fast, its main defense is its cartilage-covered backside. If threatened, a wombat will run to its burrow and block the entrance with its rump, which acts like a shield. If the intruder gets past the entrance, the wombat uses its tough bottom to crush the intruder against the burrow roof.

Question 46

True or false?
A female lion is a better hunter
than a male lion.

Question 46
True or false? A female lion is a better hunter than a male lion.

Answer: True

A female lion is called a lioness. She is smaller and leaner than a male lion, so she is more agile and can run faster to catch **prey**. Another reason that a lioness makes a better hunter is that she has no mane. If a male lion had to run around chasing prey in the hot African sunshine, he would become overheated because of his thick mane. A lioness is better able to withstand the heat while out on the hunt since she does not have a heavy mane around her head and shoulders.

The honey possum is called a(n)
_____ because it drinks nectar.

Question 47

The honey possum is called a(n) _____ because it drinks nectar.

Answer: nectarivore

The honey possum looks like a grayish-brown mouse with a pointy nose and a very long tail. Despite the name, it is not actually an opossum, though it has a similar body shape and, like an opossum, is a marsupial. The honey possum lives within a small region of Australia, feeding only on the nectar and pollen from flowering plants. It has a long tongue with little bristles at the tip, which help it collect the nectar and pollen from each flower it finds. Even though the honey possum is so small, it plays a big role in pollinating many plants.

Question 48

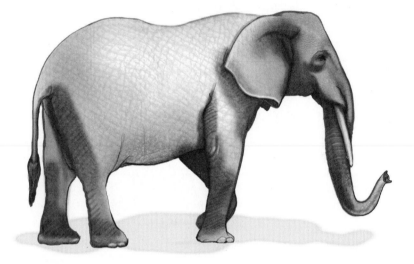

How many different species of elephants are there?

Question 48
How many different species of elephants are there?

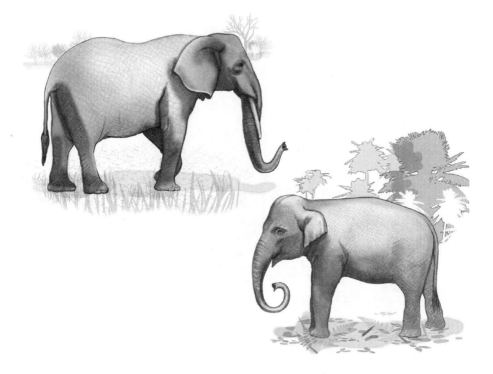

Answer: Two

Though still open to debate, it is generally agreed that there are two main species of elephants: African and Asian. Named for the continents on which they live, each of these two main elephant species are divided into several subspecies based on habitat and physical features. The easiest way to tell the difference between an African and Asian elephant is by their ears. An African elephant has larger ears, which are shaped like the continent of Africa. An Asian elephant has smaller, more droopy ears. African elephants are also generally larger than Asian elephants.

Question 49

Galagos are classified as which
of the following?

a) Marsupials
b) Primates
c) Rodents
d) Insectivores

Galagos are classified as which of the following?

Answer: b) Primates

Though many galagos look like tree squirrels, they are actually **primates**, along with apes and monkeys. There are about 20 known species of galagos. Some are as small as a mouse and larger ones are the size of a cat. All galagos share the same basic features: large, round eyes; bat-like ears; and long, furry tails. Native to Africa, galagos spend most of their lives in trees and are **nocturnal**, meaning that they are active at night. Galagos are also known as bush babies because of their distinctive calls, which sound like a crying baby.

True or false?
The Tasmanian devil gets its name from
the two little horns on top of its head.

Question 50
True or false? The Tasmanian devil gets its name from the two little horns on top of its head.

Answer: False

The Tasmanian devil does not have horns. Native to the Australian island of Tasmania, this bad-tempered mammal comes out at night to feed. Its screams and growls sound especially spooky in the dark, which is why early settlers called them "devils." A Tasmanian devil looks like a cross between a small dog and a rodent, but it is actually the largest carnivorous marsupial, meaning that it eats meat and carries its babies in a pouch. As a **carnivore,** the Tasmanian devil has sharp teeth and powerful jaws that are strong enough to bite through bones.

Question 51

The _____ looks like it has a pig's snout, a rabbit's ears, and a kangaroo's tail.

Question 51

The _____ looks like it has a pig's snout, a rabbit's ears, and a kangaroo's tail.

Answer: aardvark

Aardvark is a South African word that means "earth pig." The aardvark eats mostly ants and termites, which it sniffs out with its pig-like snout and collects on its long, sticky tongue. Because it has poor eyesight, the aardvark relies on its keen sense of hearing in order to avoid **predators** like lions and hyenas. It can hide from danger by digging itself a burrow in as little as 30 seconds. If an aardvark needs to fight off a predator, it can scratch with its tough claws or use its muscular tail like a whip. Ouch!

How many hours a day does a koala sleep?

Question 52
How many hours a day does a koala sleep?

Answer: About 20 hours a day

A koala sleeps so much because of the food it eats. Koalas are native to eastern Australia, where their primary food source is eucalyptus leaves. These leaves are actually poisonous to other animals, but not to koalas. In a 24-hour day, a koala spends about four hours eating (usually at night), and spends the rest of the time sleeping. A koala sleeps so much because its body needs time and energy to properly digest the fibrous eucalyptus leaves. Koalas are sometimes referred to as "koala bears" because of their bear-like appearance, but they are actually marsupials.

Question 53

The rock hyrax is a(n) _____ mammal, meaning that it is active during the day.

Question 53

The rock hyrax is a(n) _____ mammal, meaning that it is active during the day.

Answer: diurnal

The rock hyrax looks like a pudgy rabbit with small, rounded ears and thin, stumpy legs. Native to Africa, the rock hyrax is active during the day, and spends most of its time soaking up the warm sunshine. At night, it returns to its nest to sleep. The rock hyrax does not burrow, but instead makes its home among boulders or in rock crevices. The bottoms of its feet have a rubbery texture that stays slightly damp with sweat, so a rock hyrax's feet act like little suction cups to keep it from slipping on rocky surfaces.

Question 54

True or false?
Kangaroo and wallaby are two
different names for the same mammal.

Question 54
True or false? Kangaroo and wallaby are two different names for the same mammal.

Answer: False

Though similar, kangaroos and wallabies are two different marsupials in the **macropod** family, which comes from the word for "large feet" in Latin. Macropods are best known for how they move around by hopping. The main differences between kangaroos and wallabies are their size, legs, and teeth. A kangaroo is generally much larger than a wallaby. While a kangaroo's muscular hind legs are built for speed on open ground, a wallaby's hind legs are smaller and more agile for moving through forest areas. A kangaroo has teeth designed for biting tufts of grass, whereas a wallaby has teeth made for grinding leaves.

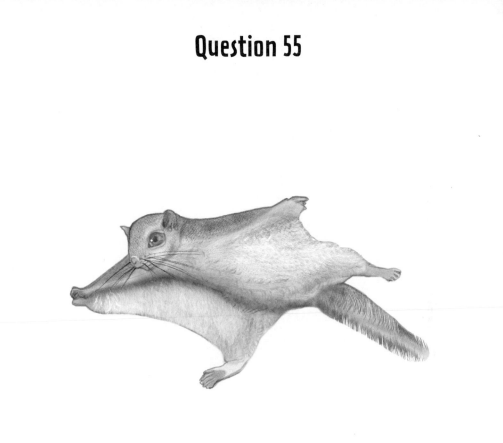

How far can a sugar glider "fly"?

Question 55
How far can a sugar glider "fly"?

Answer: About 150 ft, which is about 46 m

This is almost the width of a football field. A sugar glider has a flap of skin, called a **membrane**, on either side of its body that connects between its front and hind legs. To move from tree to tree, a sugar glider jumps and spreads out all four legs, which stretches the membranes. A sugar glider does not actually fly, but when it jumps and the stretched membranes catch the air, it glides as if it were flying. A marsupial, the sugar glider is a type of opossum and gets it name from its favorite food—sugary sweet nectar from flowers.

Chapter 6

Under the Sea

Under the Sea

While most mammals live primarily on land, some spend most or all of their lives in the water. These are known as aquatic mammals, based on the Latin word for "water;" they may live in freshwater habitats such as rivers and lakes, or in the ocean, which is salt water. Aquatic mammals that live primarily in the ocean are called **marine** mammals; marine comes from the Latin word for "sea." They can be found in all five of the world's ocean regions: Pacific, Atlantic, Arctic, Indian, and Southern. Dive in and discover the underwater world of these amazing mammals.

Which of these is not a marine mammal?

a) Polar bear
b) Seal
c) Penguin
d) Whale

Question 56
Which of these is not a marine mammal?

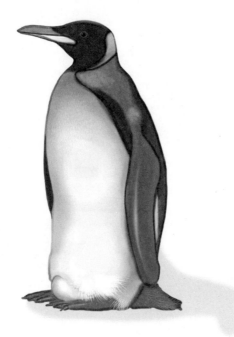

Answer: c) Penguin

Marine mammals can be found in all five of the world's oceans. These mammals come in all shapes and sizes—furry polar bears; sleek, fat seals; and gigantic whales. Though they look very different from land mammals, marine mammals still have the three key mammalian features: they have some form of hair or fur, they have three middle ear bones, and the females produce **milk** to feed their babies. Though a penguin might look furry like a polar bear and swim like a seal, a penguin is a bird, not a mammal.

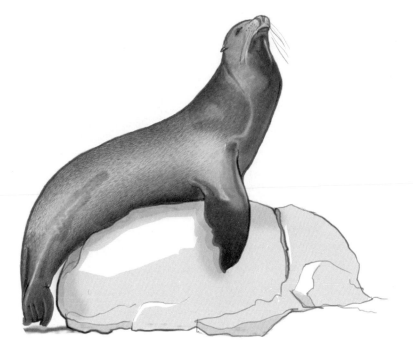

Marine mammals that have foot-like flippers are called _____ .

Question 57
Marine mammals that have foot-like flippers are called _____ .

Answer: pinnipeds

The word *pinniped* means "fin foot" in Latin. Pinnipeds include seals, sea lions, and walruses; these marine mammals have four **limbs** called **flippers**. Flippers are often confused with fins. The difference is that flippers have bones and joints, whereas fins do not. Some marine mammals, such as dolphins, have both flippers and fins. What is unique about pinnipeds is that they only have flippers, arranged in two sets just like the front and hind legs of land mammals. Though flippers are mainly used for swimming, pinnipeds are able to use them to "walk" on land, though it looks more like a waddle.

True or false?
All marine mammals have hair or fur.

Question 58
True or false? All marine mammals have hair or fur.

Answer: True

One of the main features that defines a mammal is hair or fur. This is easy to see on some marine mammals, such as a sea otter's thick fur or a walrus's hairy mustache. But even slippery dolphins and smooth-skinned whales have hair. These marine mammals are born with tiny hairs on their snout, or **rostrum**. Most dolphins and whales lose these tiny hairs shortly after birth, though some species still have rostrum hairs as adults. For example, if you have ever seen a humpback whale up close, the large bumps around its mouth are actually hair follicles.

Question 59

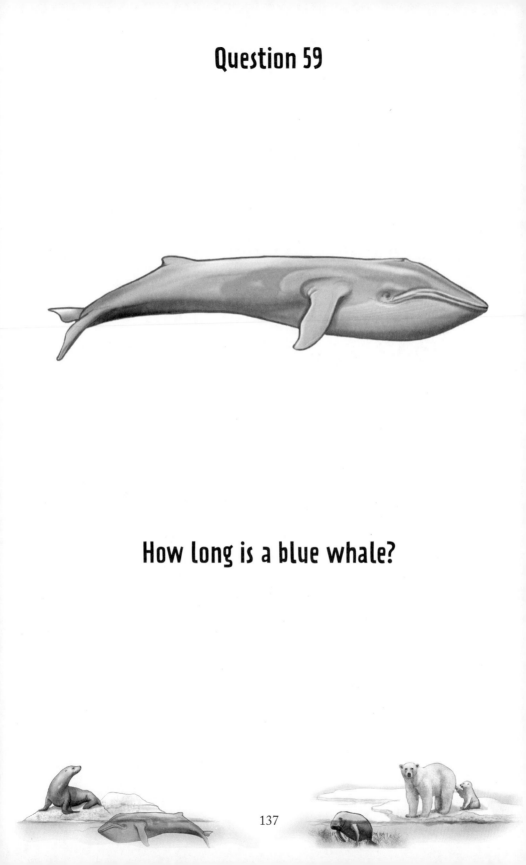

How long is a blue whale?

Question 59
How long is a blue whale?

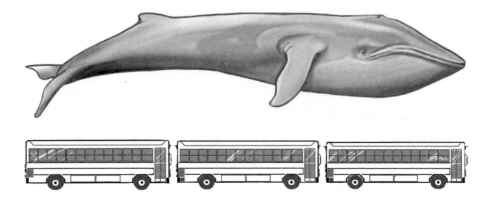

Answer: About 110 ft long, which is about 34 m

The blue whale is the largest mammal in the world, and the largest animal ever to have lived—even bigger than dinosaurs! An adult blue whale can be as long as three school buses parked end-to-end. Unlike most other mammals, female blue whales are larger than males. The blue whale lives in all of the world's oceans, except for the Arctic. It feeds on tiny, shrimp-like creatures called krill. Instead of teeth, the blue whale has rows of thick, long bristles called **baleen**. To eat, a blue whale takes a huge mouthful of water and then uses the baleen like a filter to catch all the krill, which it then swallows.

Which of the following describes sea lions' habit of floating on the water as a group?

a) Huddling
b) Rafting
c) Bonding
d) Gabbing

Question 60
Which of the following describes sea lions' habit of floating on the water as a group?

Answer: b) Rafting

If sea lions are unable to find a suitable spot on land to rest or sleep, they will often float in the water together as a group, called a **raft**. As the rafting sea lions float, each one raises a flipper to help regulate its body temperature. With a flipper in the air, a sea lion can either absorb or release heat, depending on what its body needs. From a distance, a raft of sea lions with their flippers in the air might look like they are ill or in distress, but they are most likely just resting.

A polar bear is considered a marine mammal because it lives on _____ .

Question 61
A polar bear is considered a marine mammal because it lives on _____ .

Answer: sea ice

If you look at a globe, the area around the top is called the Arctic Circle. It is so cold in the Arctic Circle that even the ocean water freezes, producing raft-like pieces of ice that are large enough for animals to live on. Though the polar bear is usually born on land, it spends most of its life on **sea ice**. Polar bears travel long distances across sea ice to find new areas for hunting seals. The polar bear is the largest of all bear species, and it stays warm by having a thick layer of **blubber**, or fat, underneath its dense coat.

Question 62

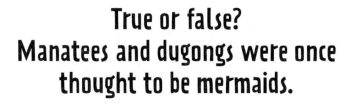

True or false?
Manatees and dugongs were once
thought to be mermaids.

Question 62
True or false? Manatees and dugongs were once thought to be mermaids.

Answer: True

Manatees and dugongs make up a group of **aquatic** mammals called sirenians. This name comes from "siren," a type of creature in Greek mythology that inspired the idea of mermaids. While Christopher Columbus was sailing to the New World, he recorded in his journal that he had seen three mermaids, but that they were "not half as beautiful as they are painted." It is now believed that what Columbus actually saw were manatees. These gentle, graceful mammals are **herbivores**; because most of their diet consists of underwater plants and grasses, they are also known as "sea cows."

Question 63

What feature do dolphins and porpoises have in common?

a) Method of communication
b) Sociability
c) Sense of smell
d) Lifespan

Question 63
What feature do dolphins and porpoises have in common?

Answer: c) Sense of smell

Though closely related, dolphins and porpoises belong to two separate families of marine mammals. Compared to porpoises, dolphins make more sounds to communicate, live in larger pods, and have longer lifespans. But one thing that dolphins and porpoises have in common is their sense of smell, or rather, the total lack of it. This is because their brain does not have an **olfactory lobe**, which controls the ability to smell. Though they lack the sense of smell, dolphins and porpoises make up for it with their excellent sense of hearing, which helps them navigate their underwater world.

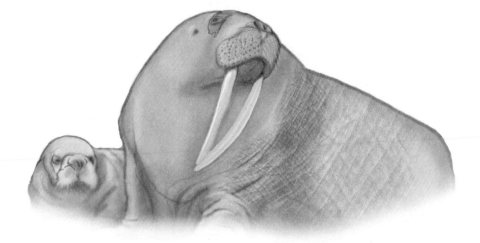

When walruses leave the water and pull themselves onto ice or land, this is called _____.

Question 64
When walruses leave the water and pull themselves onto ice or land, this is called _____.

Answer: hauling out

When walruses need to rest or tend to their young, they leave the water. Walruses prefer **hauling out** onto sea ice, but depending on their location, they may choose to haul out onto land. Though a walrus can weigh as much as a small car, it uses its strong ivory **tusks** to help pull itself out of the water. This is why the Latin name for the walrus translates as "tooth-walking sea horse." Walruses are very social mammals and usually haul out as an entire herd, which can number in the hundreds or thousands.

True or false?
The killer whale is a member of
the dolphin family.

Question 65

True or false? The killer whale is a member of the dolphin family.

Answer: True

The killer whale is properly known as an orca. Sailors of long ago gave orcas the nickname "killer of whales" after seeing them attack and kill other whales and even great white sharks. Over time, the nickname was shortened to "killer whale," which has since caused confusion because the orca is actually the largest member of the dolphin family. Orcas belong to the dolphin family because of several distinctive features: cone-shaped teeth; one blowhole instead of two; and a special organ in its head, called the **melon**, that helps the orca hear sounds under water.

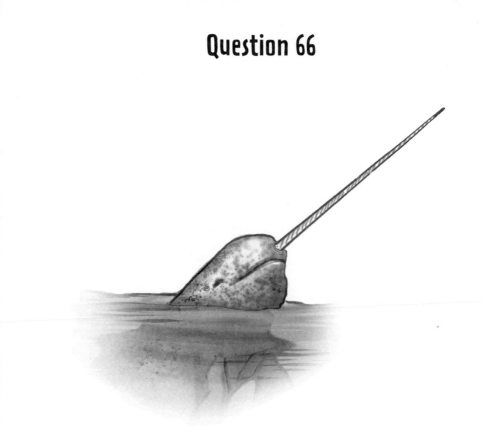

The horn-like spire that grows out of a narwhal's head is actually which of these?

a) Tooth
b) Bone
c) Nail
d) Horn

Question 66

The horn-like spire that grows out of a narwhal's head is actually which of these?

Answer: a) Tooth

Known as "the unicorn of the sea," a narwhal is a whale with a long, spiraled tooth, or tusk, on its head. A narwhal only has two teeth, but neither of them are inside its mouth. One tooth never grows through the gumline, and the other tooth grows straight out the front of its head. The narwhal's tusk is about as long as an average fishing rod. A narwhal uses its tusk to sense its surroundings and to "swat" fish to stun them before eating them. Because a narwhal has no teeth in its mouth, it must swallow its food whole.

Chapter 7

Across the Plains

Across the Plains

A plain is a large area of land that is relatively flat. Some plains are so vast that they span across different countries, like the Great Plains of North America. Plains may be cold, such as the steppes of Eurasia, or they may be hot, like those in Africa. Besides being flat, plains have sparse vegetation and very few trees. Small mammals may burrow in the ground or make nests in the grass, but large mammals must always be on the lookout because they have no way of hiding themselves. Venture out to the world's wide open spaces and explore the mammals of the plains. As you will see, there is nothing "plain" about them.

Question 67

How fast can a cheetah run?

Question 67
How fast can a cheetah run?

Answer: About 75 mi, or 120 km, per hour

As the world's fastest land mammal, the cheetah can reach sprinting speeds equal to that of cars driving on a freeway. Though a cheetah can run this fast, it cannot maintain such speed for a long time. A cheetah only runs at this speed for less than a minute while hunting, allowing it to overtake its **prey**. With its long and flexible spine, a cheetah can fully extend its front and hind legs in order to take extra long strides. A cheetah can cover almost the length of a school bus in a single stride.

Question 68

What is the fennec fox's most notable feature?

a) Tail
b) Ears
c) Fur
d) Paws

Question 68
What is the fennec fox's most notable feature?

Answer: b) Ears

About the size of a Chihuahua, the fennec fox is the world's smallest wild **canine**. It is known for its enormous ears, which are about the size of a child's hand. The fennec fox gets rid of extra body heat through these large, bat-like ears, which help keep the fox cool in the hot deserts of North Africa. Its oversized ears are also very sensitive to sound—the fennec fox is actually able to hear its prey underneath the sand. This allows it to dig in just the right spot to find food such as grasshoppers, lizards, and small rodents.

Question 69

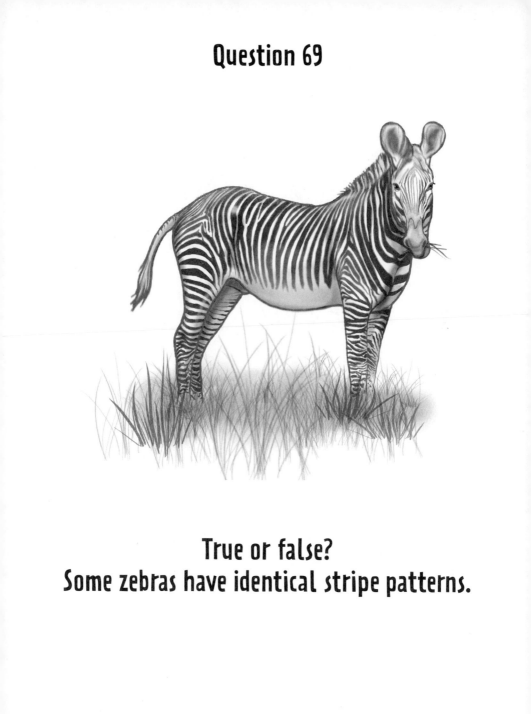

True or false?
Some zebras have identical stripe patterns.

Question 69
True or false? Some zebras have identical stripe patterns.

Answer: False

There are three different species of zebras: the plains zebra, the mountain zebra, and Grevy's zebra. Each species lives in a different area of Africa and has its own stripe pattern. Even within the same species, though, no two zebras have identical stripes, just as no two people have identical thumbprints. While it was once thought that a zebra's stripes helped it to **camouflage** in tall grass, research now shows that the stripes actually repel flies because the black-and-white pattern confuses them. Zebras belong to the horse family, but have never been **domesticated**.

The mongoose, a relative of the meerkat, is known for being able to kill venomous _____.

Question 70
The mongoose, a relative of the meerkat, is known for being able to kill venomous _____.

Answer: snakes

Like its relative the meerkat, the mongoose is a small **carnivore**, preying on rodents, birds, insects, and reptiles. In particular, the Indian gray mongoose is best known for preying on venomous snakes, especially cobras. A fierce fighter and quick killer, the Indian gray mongoose can withstand venomous snake bites because its body is immune to the **venom**. Some families in India actually keep a mongoose as a pet to make sure their home stays free of snakes. The mongoose is a **crepuscular** mammal, meaning that it is most active at dawn and at dusk.

Question 71

How long is a giraffe's neck?

Question 71
How long is a giraffe's neck?

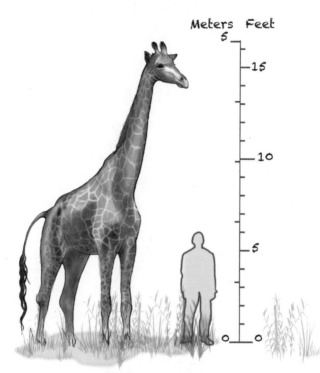

Meters Feet

Answer: About 6 ft long, which is almost 2 m

Native to the savannas of Africa, the giraffe is the world's tallest mammal. A giraffe's neck measures a little more than the height of an average man, and its legs are equally as long. All together, an adult giraffe stands tall enough to look through a second-story window. Despite its long neck, a giraffe has trouble reaching down to the ground because of its long legs. This is why a giraffe prefers to eat tree leaves. Staying upright to eat, sleep, and even while giving birth allows a giraffe to see any approaching **predators**.

Question 72

True or false?
Gophers cause soil damage.

Question 72
True or false? Gophers cause soil damage.

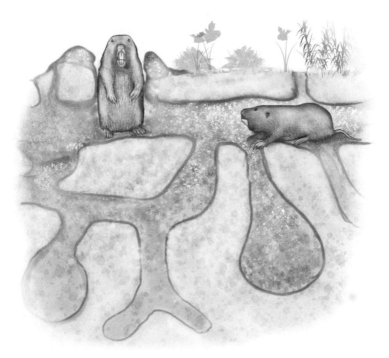

Answer: False

Gophers are **fossorial**, which means "digging" in Latin; they spend most of their time underground making tunnels. Properly known as pocket gophers, they are called such because of the pouches of fur-lined skin on the outside of their cheeks. As gophers tunnel underground, they store bits of food or nesting material in their cheek pockets. Gophers dig their tunnels into extensive networks which can disrupt plant roots, so gardeners and farmers have to protect their property from gophers. Despite this, these tunneling rodents play an important part in keeping the soil healthy by mixing and loosening it.

After becoming extinct in the wild, the Arabian oryx was re-bred and let into the wild again; this is called _____.

Question 73

After becoming extinct in the wild, the Arabian oryx was re-bred and let into the wild again; this is called _____.

Answer: reintroduction

The Arabian oryx is a type of antelope found in the hot, dry plains of the Middle East. It has a white coat with dark brown legs, and two long horns that slightly curve toward its back. Just fifty years ago, the Arabian oryx could only be found in captivity and was declared **extinct** in the wild due to uncontrolled capture and hunting. Thanks to a successful zoo-based breeding program called "Operation Oryx," the species was **reintroduced** into the wild and herds can once again be found in the Middle East.

Question 74

How wide can a hippo open its mouth?

169

Question 74
How wide can a hippo open its mouth?

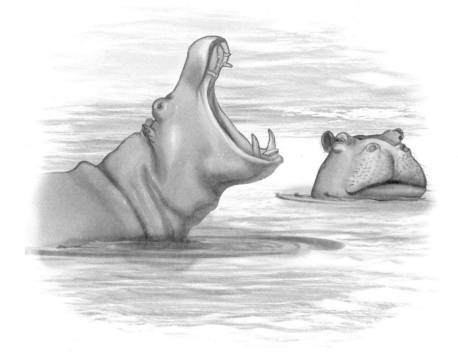

Answer: About 4 ft, which is over 1 m

With the largest mouth of any land mammal, a hippopotamus, or hippo for short, can open its mouth to an angle of almost 180 degrees. This behavior is called "gaping." The biggest male hippo of a group will often gape to show that he is in charge, or to frighten away predators. Hippos are **semi-aquatic** mammals, meaning that they spend a lot of time in the water. Though hippos are **herbivores**, their sharp **tusks**, powerful jaws, and aggressive habits can be a deadly combination. As many as 3,000 people in Africa are killed each year in hippo attacks.

Question 75

Which of the following animals is the main food source for the black-footed ferret?

a) Prairie dog
b) Grouse
c) Prairie chicken
d) Rabbit

Question 75
Which of the following animals is the main food source for the black-footed ferret?

Answer: a) Prairie dog

The prairie dog, a type of large ground squirrel, is the primary food source for the black-footed ferret. Both prey and predator are about the same size, so a black-footed ferret can easily enter a prairie dog burrow and hunt it in its own home. Because of its sneaky hunting habits and its facial markings, the black-footed ferret is known as the "masked bandit" of the American plains. As North America's only ferret species, the black-footed ferret plays an important part in maintaining the balance of its natural **habitat** by keeping prairie dogs from **overpopulating**.

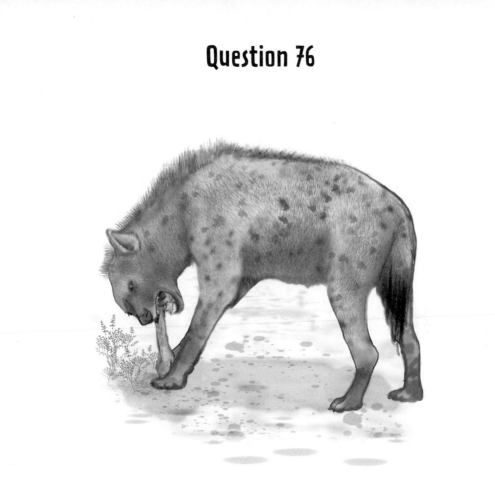

True or false?
The hyena is a member of the canine family.

Question 76
True or false? The hyena is a member of the canine family.

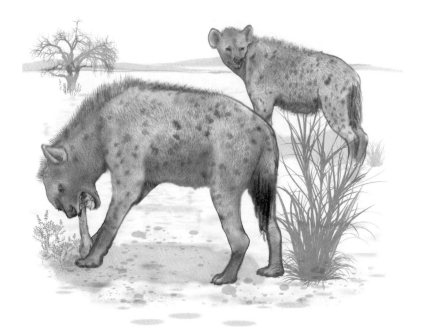

Answer: False

Though the hyena looks like a type of wild dog, it actually belongs to its own family of carnivores, Hyaenidae. There are four species in the hyena family; they are native to Africa and parts of Asia. Though hyenas primarily **scavenge** off of other predators' prey, they will also hunt, either by themselves or in a **pack**. With their powerful jaws and strong teeth, hyenas can eat practically every part of their prey, including bones, fur, and teeth. The term "laughing hyena" came about because one species, the spotted hyena, makes a giggling sound, but not because it is happy—it "laughs" when it is threatened or under attack!

Question 77

How long can a camel go without water?

Question 77
How long can a camel go without water?

Answer: About seven months

There are two types of camels: the dromedary has one hump and the Bactrian has two. Though a camel can go about seven months without drinking water, this is usually in extreme circumstances. Generally, a camel gets moisture from the plants it eats. When a camel does drink, it can take in as much as a bathtub full of water in three minutes. Many people think that camels' humps store water. In fact, camels' humps are made of fat. If food or water is scarce, camels can use the fat in their humps as "fuel" for their bodies.

Chapter 8

The Marvel of Motherhood

The Marvel of Motherhood

All mammals, from the humble rat to the magnificent blue whale, have very similar beginnings. Before birth, they are carried inside their mother's body while they develop. Mammals are born at different levels of maturity. Most hoofed mammals are up and walking soon after birth, whereas primates are born almost completely helpless. Some mammals, like dolphins, only have one baby at a time. Other mammals, such as pigs, give birth to a whole group. After being born, mammal babies rely on their mother's care, which includes feeding, protecting, and teaching survival skills. Read on to learn how mammal moms make sure their young can thrive in a big world.

Question 78

Which of these words describes the period of time that a mammal mother carries her unborn young?

a) Incubation
b) Reproduction
c) Gestation
d) Maturation

Question 78

Which of these words describes the period of time that a mammal mother carries her unborn young?

Answer: c) Gestation

For humans this is called **pregnancy**, but for the rest of the mammal world, it is referred to as **gestation**. During gestation, the unborn young grows inside its mother's **uterus**, a special organ in her body which provides nutrients and protection to the developing baby. The period of time for gestation varies widely depending on the species. For some mammals, it is just a few weeks; for others, almost two years. Gestation time depends a lot on how the unborn offspring grow and develop inside the mother, which is different for each species.

True or false?
The process of gestation and birth is
the same for all mammals.

Question 79
True or false? The process of gestation and birth is the same for all mammals.

Placental

Monotreme

Marsupial

Answer: False

Mammals are divided into three groups based on their process of gestation and birth. Most mammals, including humans, are **placental**, meaning that the unborn young develops inside its mother's uterus and is nourished through an organ called the placenta. At birth, the mother pushes the baby out of her body. **Marsupials**, such as kangaroos, have a very short gestation period. The undeveloped baby then crawls into its mother's pouch, where it will feed on her **milk** continually until it is fully developed and can leave the pouch. **Monotremes**, such as platypuses, actually hatch from eggs that the mother lays.

Question 80

How long is gestation for an elephant?

183

Question 80
How long is gestation for an elephant?

Answer: Almost two years

Of all mammals, the elephant has the longest gestation, lasting nearly two years. The gestation period is so long due to the unborn elephant's physical size and brain capacity. A mother elephant almost always gives birth to a single calf; twins are rare. Because the calf is born very well developed, it can walk soon after birth, staying close to its mother and following her wherever she goes. This is why elephants are called **follow mammals**. A mother elephant's milk is low in protein and fat, so her calf must feed often.

Question 81

_____ is the first food for mammal babies.

Question 81

_____ is the first food for mammal babies.

Answer: Milk

All mammal mothers, from the smallest mouse to the largest whale, produce milk to feed their babies. This is one of the key features of being a mammal. Each mother's milk is unique to the species, having just the right amounts of fat, protein, sugar, and water for the proper development of her young. The milk also contains infection-fighting nutrients that keep the babies healthy. When a baby mammal feeds on its mother's milk, it is called **nursing** or suckling. When a human mother nurses her baby, it is also called **breastfeeding**.

Question 82

Which of these mammals is a marsupial?

a) Rat
b) Armadillo
c) Skunk
d) Kangaroo

187

Question 82
Which of these mammals is a marsupial?

Answer: d) Kangaroo

Marsupial comes from a Greek word that means "pouch." Kangaroos, koalas, and opossums are just a few of several hundred marsupial species. These mammals have a short gestation period, after which the undeveloped young crawl out of the birth canal, up their mother's abdomen, and into her pouch. Here they will nurse continually over the next several months. Marsupial babies, called joeys, cannot leave the pouch until they are more developed. Once they are old enough, joeys will emerge to explore outside and begin to sample solid foods, though they return to their mother's pouch to nurse and sleep.

True or false?
All placental mammal babies are born
with their eyes closed.

Question 83
True or false? All placental mammal babies are born with their eyes closed.

Answer: False

Some placental mammal babies are born with their eyes closed, but others are born with their eyes open. Generally, most **nest mammals** are born with their eyes closed and are completely helpless. They rely on the protection of their burrow and the warmth provided by their littermates. Once their eyes have opened, they can start exploring the world around them. Follow mammals are typically born with their eyes open and are ready to walk soon after birth. They are not kept in a nest or carried around, so the babies must be ready to travel with the mother wherever she goes.

Question 84

How many families of egg-laying mammals are there?

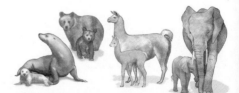

Question 84
How many families of egg-laying mammals are there?

Answer: Two

There are only two families of egg-laying mammals: the platypus and the echidna (pronounced eh-KID-na), also known as a spiny anteater. There are four species of echidna and only one species of platypus. These mammals are called monotremes, which means "single hole" in Greek. Like birds, the platypus and the echidna have only one opening through which they pass all waste and lay eggs. A female platypus usually lays two eggs at a time, while an echidna only lays one. Monotreme hatchlings are called puggles, and just like all other mammal babies, they are fed with their mother's milk.

Question 85

When a mammal mother gives birth to a group of offspring, it is called a(n) _____.

Question 85

When a mammal mother gives birth to a group of offspring, it is called a(n) _____.

Answer: litter

Mammals that are born in a **litter** are referred to as nest mammals. The mother gives birth to her litter in a protected place such as a burrow or nest. Her babies are very helpless when they are newborns and need the mother's care. Though the mother may leave between feedings, the litter stays safe and warm together in the nest. The mother's milk does not have high amounts of protein or fat, so she nurses her litter every few hours. The most well known nest mammals are rodents, **canines**, and **felines**.

Question 86

True or false?
Mammal mothers always stay with
their young to keep them safe.

195

Question 86
True or false? Mammal mothers always stay with their young to keep them safe.

Answer: False

While some mammal mothers are always with their babies, others leave their young alone for many hours at a time in a hidden place. The mother forages nearby so that she can hear if her babies call. They are safer by themselves because the mother's scent and movement may attract **predators**. This type of mammal is called a **cache mammal**. *Cache* comes from the French word which means "to hide." The mother's milk is high in protein and fat, which keeps her babies full for hours at a time. Cache mammals include various species, such as bears, deer, and rabbits.

Question 87

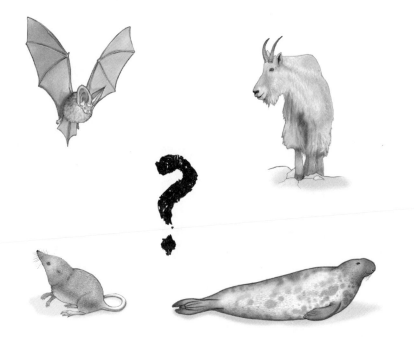

Which mammal nurses its young for only four days?

a) Pygmy shrew
b) Hooded seal
c) Gray bat
d) Mountain goat

197

Question 87
Which mammal nurses its young for only four days?

Answer: b) Hooded seal

The hooded seal lives in the Arctic, where it spends most of its time diving deep underwater for food. Hooded seal pups are born on the ice and must build up a layer of **blubber** very quickly in order to survive the Arctic's harsh conditions. Over a four-day nursing period, the pup drinks so much milk that its body doubles in size. The mother's milk is 60% fat, which is the highest fat content of all mammal milk; by comparison, cow's milk is just over 3% fat. The hooded seal has the shortest nursing period of all mammals.

Question 88

How long does an orangutan baby nurse
before being fully weaned?

199

Question 88
How long does an orangutan baby nurse before being fully weaned?

Answer: About seven years

The orangutan has the longest nursing period of any mammal. This is because the baby has a slow rate of growth and development. Even though it is born with its eyes open, an orangutan baby is completely helpless and relies on its mother for warmth, food, protection, and transportation. The mother must carry her baby wherever she goes. For this reason, an orangutan is called a **carry mammal**. The mother's milk is low in protein and fat, so she must nurse her baby throughout the day and night. An orangutan baby is not fully **weaned** until it is about seven years old.

Chapter 9

Weird and Wild

Weird and Wild

In this book, you have traveled all around the world—from the plains of Africa to the rainforests of South America, from high in the mountains to deep in the ocean— exploring all kinds of mammals and how they live. Now you know why a donkey is thought to be stubborn, how a sloth is able to camouflage itself, and what a hippo does to scare away predators. There is no end to learning about the wonderful world of mammals. Here are some final facts to add to what you already know. For example, which mammal can walk on water? Turn the page and find out!

Though the pangolin is a mammal, it looks more like a reptile because its skin is covered in _____.

Question 89

Though the pangolin is a mammal, it looks more like a reptile because its skin is covered in _____.

Answer: scales

The pangolin is the only mammal in the world that has scales covering its skin. These scales are used for protection when a pangolin is threatened. A pangolin's scales are made of **keratin**, which is the same material that makes up your fingernails. Also known as scaly anteaters, there are eight species of pangolins: four are native to Asia and four are native to Africa. Some species are tree-dwellers in forest areas, while other species live on the ground in savannas. If a pangolin feels threatened, it curls itself up into a tight, armor-like ball and waits for the danger to pass.

Question 90

Which of these mammals can walk on water?

a) Water shrew
b) Muskrat
c) River otter
d) Platypus

Question 90
Which of these mammals can walk on water?

Answer: a) Water shrew

The water shrew looks like a large mouse with a long, pointy nose. It lives near ponds, lakes, streams, and rivers, and is considered an **insectivore** because it mainly eats insects. The water shrew has fringes of stiff hair on its feet, which trap air bubbles and allow it to run across the surface of the water. A water shrew can also dive underwater in search of food. But because air bubbles get trapped in its thick fur, it must dive and swim quickly to avoid floating to the water's surface.

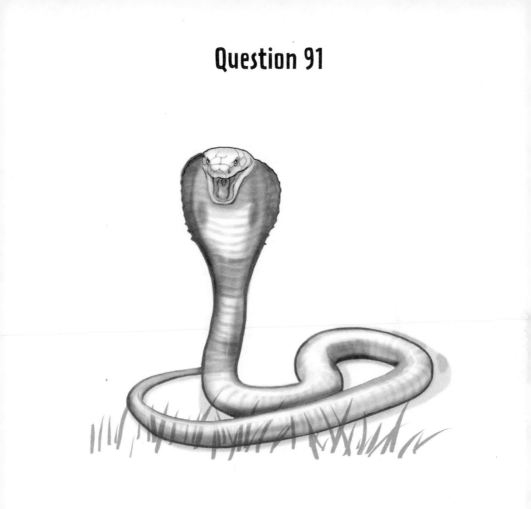

True or false?
Some mammals are venomous.

Question 91
True or false? Some mammals are venomous.

Answer: True

While the term "venomous" brings to mind snakes and spiders, there are a handful of mammals that are venomous. **Venom** is a toxic substance released directly into the bloodstream, not to be confused with poison, which enters the body by touching, eating, or breathing. Most venomous mammals release their venom by biting, such as the shrew-like solenodon and the slow loris, a **primate**. The platypus is the only venomous mammal that does not bite in order to release its venom. Specific to the male platypus, it has a claw-like **spur** above each hind foot, which releases venom when stabbed into another animal.

Question 92

Which of these mammals is the most dangerous to humans?

a) Grizzly bear
b) Killer whale
c) Domestic dog
d) Wild boar

Question 92
Which of these mammals is the most dangerous to humans?

Answer: c) Domestic dog

Unfortunately, "man's best friend" can also be man's worst enemy. About 60,000 people worldwide die each year from bites by rabies-infected dogs. Though the United States has a very low incidence of rabies, well over 300,000 people each year end up in the emergency room because of dog bites. Our **canine** friends make wonderful pets, but the fact is they are still mammals with the natural instinct to attack if they feel threatened. If you have a dog, always treat it with respect and care. If you want to pet a dog that is not your own, always ask the owner's permission first.

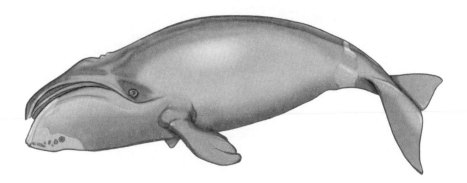

How long can a bowhead whale live?

Question 93
How long can a bowhead whale live?

Answer: About 200 years

The bowhead whale is the world's longest-living mammal, with an average lifespan of 200 years. This means that a 200-year-old bowhead whale alive today was born when Abraham Lincoln was a boy. The bowhead whale gets its name from the distinctive curve of its mouth, which is shaped like an archer's bow. Making its home in the icy waters around the Arctic Circle, the bowhead whale has the thickest **blubber** of any whale species. When a bowhead whale needs to come up for air, its huge, triangular skull is strong enough to break right through the Arctic ice.

Some mammals are social and live in groups; others are _____ and live alone.

Question 94

Some mammals are social and live in groups; others are _____ and live alone.

Answer: solitary

Some mammals, such as monkeys and dolphins, live in large groups, thriving on interaction among the members. These are called **social mammals**. The goal of social mammals is to raise their young to be **interdependent** on the other members of their group, which is how they best survive. Other mammals, such as bears and sloths, live by themselves or in very small groups, such as a mother and her babies. These are called **solitary mammals**. The goal of solitary mammals is to raise their young to be **independent**, capable of surviving on their own.

Question 95

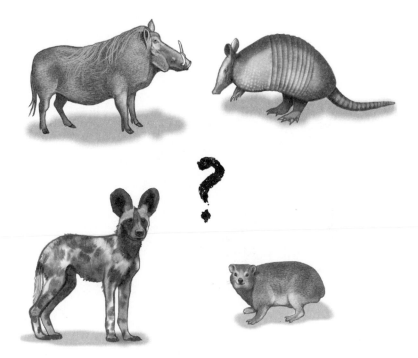

Which mammal always gives birth to identical quadruplets?

a) Common warthog
b) Nine-banded armadillo
c) African wild dog
d) Rock hyrax

Question 95
Which mammal always gives birth to identical quadruplets?

Answer: b) Nine-banded armadillo

The nine-banded armadillo gets its name from the number of armor bands covering its midsection. This armadillo species is unique among other armadillos because the mother always gives birth to identical quadruplets. During early **gestation**, the single egg cell splits into four identical cells, each of which develops into a baby armadillo. Each **litter** of four armadillo pups are either all males or all females. The pups are born well developed, but because their armor is still soft, they stay safe in their burrow for a few weeks before leaving to explore.

True or false?
The Old English Sheepdog is now an endangered breed.

Question 96
True or false? The Old English Sheepdog is now an endangered breed.

Answer: True

Known for its fluffy coat, the Old English Sheepdog was originally bred as a working dog in rural England. This breed was typically used to help men called "drovers" move livestock from farm to market, which often took many days on foot. The Old English Sheepdog's loyal temperament made it a trustworthy companion, and its wool-like fur kept it warm and dry on the long journey. With changes in farming practices and more people now living in cities, there has been a dramatic downturn in demand for Old English Sheepdogs. Breeders fear this could eventually lead to the dog's **extinction**.

Question 97

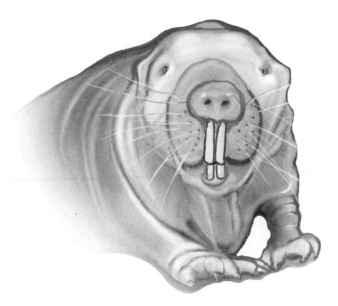

How long can a naked mole rat live?

Question 97
How long can a naked mole rat live?

Answer: Up to 30 years

The naked mole rat can live up to 30 years, which is the longest lifespan of all rodents. In fact, scientists are still researching to find out how naked mole rats live so long and never seem to age. These pink-skinned, wrinkly rodents are neither moles nor rats; they are their own species, native to the deserts and savannas of eastern Africa. As f**Fossorial** rodents, naked mole rats spend most of their lives underground, creating networks of tunnels and chambers for their colony. They even find their food underground, feeding on the water-filled roots of desert plants, called succulents.

The name of the Bactrian camel is capitalized because it is based on the name of which of these?

a) The explorer who discovered it
b) The bacteria it carries
c) The region it originally lived in
d) The feature of having two humps

Question 98
The name of the Bactrian camel is capitalized because it is based on the name of which of these?

Answer: c) The region it originally lived in

People are often confused about why *Bactrian* is capitalized, while *dromedary* is not. The two-humped Bactrian camel is named for the ancient region of Bactria, which is now part of modern-day Afghanistan. The one-humped dromedary camel gets its name from the Greek word *dromad*, meaning "runner." Because *dromedary* comes from another word, it is not capitalized. On the other hand, *Bactrian* comes from the name of a geographic region, so it is capitalized. This rule also applies to mammals named for people. For example, Hector's dolphin is named for Sir James Hector, the scientist who first described the species.

True or false?
Monkeys only eat bananas.

Question 99
True or false? Monkeys only eat bananas.

Answer: False

Though monkeys are commonly portrayed as eating bananas, they actually eat a variety of foods, including meat. In fact, research now shows that most primates eat some form of meat. The frequency, amount, and type of meat consumed depends on the primate species. For example, vervet monkeys primarily eat plants, but will occasionally eat eggs, birds, or rodents. In contrast, baboons are opportunistic eaters, consuming just about anything that is edible. This includes larger forms of meat such as sheep or goats. Many African farmers consider baboons to be pests because they are known to prey on livestock.

Mammals Chart

Discover more about the mammals included in this book!

Each entry in the mammals chart includes the name of the mammal, what its babies are called, what a group made up of those mammals is called (mammals that do not live in groups are marked "solitary"), and the order and the family to which it belongs.

Each mammal entry also has a symbol next to it. This is the conservation status of the mammal. The conservation status indicates how close a species is to extinction. On this chart, "least concern" is the lowest level, and "critically endangered" is the highest. Use the legend below to check the status of each animal.

(I) Insufficient Data   (L) Least concern   (T) Near threatened

(V) Vulnerable   (E) Endangered   (C) Critically endangered

(*) Status varies depending on individual species

	Mammal	Baby	Group Name	Order	Family
(L)	aardvark	calf, cub	solitary	Tubulidentata	Orycteropodidae
(V)	anteater, giant	pup	solitary	Pilosa	Myrmecophagidae
(C)	ape	baby	shrewdness, tribe	Primates	Hominidae
(L)	armadillo, nine-banded	pup	solitary	Cingulata	Dasypodidae
(T)	bat, Kitti's hog-nosed	pup	colony	Chiroptera	Craseonycteridae
(L)	bear, American black	cub	solitary	Carnivora	Ursidae
(V)	bear, polar	cub	solitary	Carnivora	Ursidae
(I)	bear, grizzly	cub	solitary	Carnivora	Ursidae
(L)	beaver	kit	colony, family	Rodentia	Castoridae
(C)	camel, Bactrian	calf	herd	Artiodactyla	Camelidae
(L)	camel, dromedary	calf	herd	Artiodactyla	Camelidae

	Mammal	Baby	Group Name	Order	Family
L	capybara	pup	herd	Rodentia	Caviidae
L	cat [domestic]	kitten	clowder	Carnivora	Felidae
V	cheetah	cub	coalition	Carnivora	Felidae
L	cow	calf	herd	Artiodactyla	Bovidae
L	deer	fawn	herd	Artiodactyla	Cervidae
L	dog [domestic]	puppy	pack	Carnivora	Canidae
T	dog, Old English Sheepdog	puppy	pack	Carnivora	Canidae
T	dog, short-eared	pup, whelp	solitary	Carnivora	Canidae
*	dolphin, oceanic	calf	pod	Artiodactyla	Delphinidae
L	donkey	foal	drove	Perissodactyla	Equidae
V	dugong	calf	solitary	Sirenia	Dugongidae
E	elephant, African	calf	herd	Proboscidea	Elephantidae
E	elephant, Asian	calf	herd	Proboscidea	Elephantidae
L	elk	calf	gang	Artiodactyla	Cervidae
E	ferret, black-footed	kit	business	Carnivora	Mustelidae
L	fox, fennec	kit	skulk, leash	Carnivora	Canidae
*	galago	infant	family unit	Primates	Galagidae
*	giraffe	calf	tower	Artiodactyla	Giraffidae
*	goat	kid	tribe, trip	Artiodactyla	Caprinae [subfamily]
*	gopher	pup	solitary	Rodentia	Geomyidae
V	hippopotamus	calf	bloat	Artiodactyla	Hippopotamidae
L	honey possum	joey	solitary	Diprotodontia	Tarsipedidae
*	horse	foal	herd	Perissodactyla	Equidae

	Mammal	Baby	Group Name	Order	Family
(L)	human	baby	family, community, clan, tribe...	Primates	Hominidae
(L)	hyena	cub	clan, cackle	Carnivora	Hyaenidae
(L)	hyrax, rock	pup	colony	Hyracoidea	Procaviidae
(L)	kangaroo	joey	mob	Diprotodontia	Macropodidae
(E)	koala	joey	solitary	Diprotodontia	Phascolarctidae
(V)	lion	cub	pride	Carnivora	Felidae
(L)	llama	cria	herd	Artiodactyla	Camelidae
(V)	manatee	calf	aggregation	Sirenia	Trichechidae
(*)	marmot	pup	colony	Rodentia	Sciuridae
(L)	mongoose, Indian gray	pup	solitary	Carnivora	Herpestidae
(E)	monkey, howler	infant	troop	Primates	Atelidae
(L)	moose	moose	solitary	Artiodactyla	Cervidae
(L)	mountain lion	cub	solitary	Carnivora	Felidae
(L)	mouse [common]	pup, pinky	mischief	Rodentia	Muridae
(L)	mule	foal	pack	Perissodactyla	Equidae
(L)	narwhal	calf	blessing	Artiodactyla	Monodontidae
(*)	opossum	joey	passel	Didelphimorphia	Didelphidae
(C)	orangutan	baby, infant	solitary	Primates	Hominidae
(I)	orca	calf	pod	Artiodactyla	Delphinidae
(V)	oryx, Arabian	calf	herd	Artiodactyla	Hippotraginae [subfamily]
(E)	otter, giant	pup, kitten	bevy, raft	Carnivora	Mustelidae
(E)	otter, sea	pup, kitten	raft	Carnivora	Mustelidae
(*)	pig	piglet	drift, team	Artiodactyla	Suidae
(L)	pika	kit	colony	Lagomorpha	Ochotonidae

	Mammal	Baby	Group Name	Order	Family
T	platypus	puggle	paddle	Monotremata	Ornithorhynchus
*	porpoise	pup, calf	shoal	Artiodactyla	Phocoenidae
*	rabbit	kitten, kit	colony, fluffle	Lagomorpha	Leporidae
*	rhinocerous	calf	crash	Perissodactyla	Rhinocerotidae
C	saola	calf	solitary	Artiodactyla	Bovidae
*	sea lion	pup	raft	Carnivora	Otariidae
V	seal, hooded	pup	colony, bob	Carnivora	Phocidae
*	sheep	lamb	herd	Artiodactyla	Caprinae [subfamily]
L	sheep, bighorn	lamb	herd	Artiodactyla	Caprinae [subfamily]
L	shrew, water	pup	caravan	Eulipotyphla	Soricidae
*	sloth	slowbie	solitary	Pilosa	Megalonychidae and Bradypodidae
L	sugar glider	joey	colony	Diprotodontia	Petauridae
T	tahr, Himalayan	kid	herd	Artiodactyla	Caprinae [subfamily]
*	tapir	calf	candle	Perissodactyla	Tapiridae
E	Tasmanian devil	imp, joey	solitary	Dasyuromorphia	Dasyuridae
E	tiger	cub	streak	Carnivora	Felidae
*	wallaby	joey	mob	Diprotodontia	Macropodidae
V	walrus	calf	herd	Carnivora	Odobenidae
E	whale, blue	calf	pod	Artiodactyla	Balaenopteridae
L	whale, bowhead	calf	pod	Artiodactyla	Balaenidae
L	wolf, gray	pup	pack	Carnivora	Canidae
L	wolverine	kit, cub	solitary	Carnivora	Mustelidae
*	wombat	joey	wisdom	Diprotodontia	Vombatidae
*	zebra	foal	dazzle	Perissodactyla	Equidae
L	zebu	calf	herd	Artiodactyla	Bovidae

Glossary

Apex predator: the animal at the highest point of the food chain, having no natural predators

Aquatic: growing or living in or near water

Baleen: the flexible bristles of keratin lining the upper jaws of toothless whales, used for filtering food out of ocean water

Blubber: the thick layer of fat beneath the skin of large marine mammals, such as whales, seals, and polar bears

Breastfeed: to feed a baby milk directly from the breasts; used to describe the baby being fed as well as the mother feeding the baby

Cache mammal: a mammal that hides its young in a safe place between feedings

Camouflage: to hide by disguising appearance; for mammals, this means hiding in surroundings that mimic their coat pattern or color

Canine: a member of the dog family

Carnivore: an animal that eats the meat of other animals

Carry mammal: a mammal that carries its young wherever it goes

Classification: the scientific ordering of living organisms into groups based on specific criteria

Colony: a group of animals of the same species that live together and depend on each other for their existence

Crepuscular: most active at dawn and at dusk

Dewlap: a loose fold of skin around the neck of certain animals

Diurnal: most active during the day

Domestication: the process by which a wild species is tamed or trained to rely on human care

Endemic: native to a specific region

Extinct: no longer in existence; having no living members

Feline: a member of the cat family, which is divided into two groups: big cats, such as lions and tigers, and small cats, such as ocelots and house cats

Fleece: the coat of wool-bearing mammals, especially sheep and goats

Flipper: one of the wide, flat limbs of certain marine mammals, arranged in pairs of two or four and used for swimming

Follow mammal: a mammal whose young follows closely wherever the mother goes

Food chain: a series of living organisms in which each becomes food for the next

Fossorial: living mostly underground, characterized by digging and burrowing

Frugivore: an animal that feeds primarily on fruit

Gestation: the length of time in which mammalian offspring develop in the mother's uterus before birth

Habitat: the specific geographic location or type of landscape in which a mammal or other organism lives

Hauling out: the habit of pinnipeds, such as seals and sea lions, in which they temporarily leave the water to rest on land or ice

Herbivore: an animal that feeds only on plant material

Hibernate: to spend the winter in a dormant or inactive state of low metabolism in order to save energy

Hybrid: the offspring of two animals that are of different species or breeds

Independent: not reliant on a group in order to thrive, especially among solitary mammals

Insectivore: an animal that feeds primarily on insects

Interdependent: reliant on other members of a group to survive, especially among social mammals

Invasive species: a species that is not native to and has no natural predators in an environment, thus negatively impacting the ecosystem it inhabits

Keratin: a protein that makes up body parts such as hair, fingernails, hooves, claws, and horns

Larynx: a hollow organ containing the vocal cords, found in the throat of mammals and some other animals

Limb: a jointed body part, such as an arm, leg, wing, or flipper, that is used for locomotion

Litter: multiple mammal offspring born at once to the same mother

Macropod: a member of the family of herbivorous marsupials, such as kangaroos and wallabies

Marine: of the sea or ocean

Marsupial: a type of mammal distinguished by the female's abdominal pouch, in which she carries her young after birth

Melon: a special organ in the head of toothed whales that allows them to hear under water

Membrane: a thin layer of tissue found in living organisms that may separate or protect organs, or may separate or connect different parts of the body

Milk: a fluid produced by female mammals to provide sustenance for their offspring

Monotreme: a member of the small order of egg-laying mammals, having only one opening through which the females lay eggs and pass all waste

Nectarivore: an animal that feeds mainly on the nectar of flowers

Nest mammal: a mammal that gives birth to a litter in a burrow or nest, where the young stay safe and warm

Nocturnal: most active at night

Nurse: to feed on a mother's milk; used to describe the offspring being fed as well as the mother feeding the offspring

Olfactory lobe: a section of the brain that controls a mammal's ability to smell

Omnivore: an animal that eats both plants and animals

Pack: a group of wild mammals that live and hunt together, especially canines

Pinniped: a member of the order of marine mammals that have front and rear flippers, such as seals, sea lions, and walruses

Placenta: an organ that develops along with the unborn offspring of most mammal species, providing oxygen and nutrients, and removing waste from the offspring's bloodstream during gestation

Predator: an animal that preys on other animals

Pregnancy: the length of time that a human mother carries her unborn offspring

Prehensile: capable of gripping or grasping, especially by wrapping around

Prey: an animal that is hunted by other animals for food

Primate: a member of the order of mammals that includes monkeys and apes

Proboscis: the elongated, muscular nose of some mammals that is usually flexible and capable of grabbing food or objects

Rafting: behavior exhibited by sea lions and other pinnipeds in which a group rests by floating together near the water's surface

Reintroduce: to deliberately place a species back into an area where it previously lived

Rostrum: the beak-like snout of certain animals such as dolphins, birds, and billfish

Rumen: the first chamber of the stomach in ruminants, in which food is initially broken down into cud

Ruminant: a hoofed mammal that chews the cud processed in its rumen

Sanguivore (also sanguinivore): an animal that feeds on the blood of other animals

Scavenge: to feed on garbage or the decaying meat of dead animals

Sea ice: large, floating chunks of frozen ocean water on which marine mammals live or rest

Semi-aquatic: an animal that spends much of its time in and around water, but does not live in water exclusively

Shed antlers: the antlers that fall off of a male deer each year between mid-winter and mid-spring

Social mammal: a mammal that lives in a large group of its species and is dependent on interaction with other members of the group

Solitary mammal: a mammal that lives by itself or in a very small group, such as with its offspring

Spur: a claw-like spike on the hind or front limbs of some animals, used as a defense mechanism

Symbiosis: the close interaction between two living organisms of different species, benefitting one or both

Territorial: showing behavior that defends an area within an animal's habitat

Trunk: the elongated, tubular nose of some mammals, such as elephants and tapirs

Tusk: a long, sharp tooth that protrudes from a mammal's closed mouth

Ungulate: a mammal with hooves

Uterus: the hollow organ in a female mammal that holds and protects the unborn offspring during gestation

Venom: a poisonous substance injected into a predator or prey by biting or stinging

Wean: to begin to shift a young mammal from drinking only its mother's milk to eating solid food

Wool: the soft, curly hair of sheep and goats

Index

Meet the Open Earth Team

Dia L. Michels is an award-winning science and parenting writer who has authored or edited over a dozen books for both children and adults. While her topics include science and math books for middle grade students, her passion is promoting attachment parenting and supporting breastfeeding. A popular speaker, she lectures frequently at conferences, universities, libraries, and schools around the country. The mother of three grown children, she lives in the Capitol Hill neighborhood of Washington, D.C., with five cats and a dog. She can be reached at Dia@PlatypusMedia.com.

Growing up in the home of a physician, **Bonnie Hofkin**'s first picture books and early readers were medical journals and anatomy texts. With her interest in the human body thus igniting a lifelong love of art, she first obtained a BA in commercial illustration, followed by a master's degree in medical illustration. Subsequently, she embarked on a 40+ year career as a freelance illustrator. Still going strong, her unique style, in which an eye for accuracy and visual appeal is combined with a classical look reminiscent of the great Renaissance masters, is instantly recognizable.

Though school papers were some of her most dreaded assignments as a young student, **Sarah Cox** discovered her love of wordcraft during college. Now as a researcher and writer, she has the most fun when making complex subjects understandable, especially for children. Sarah holds a BA in History and is passionate about adding historical elements to any topic. When she is not at her desk, Sarah enjoys spending time with her husband and their Scotch collie, exploring the many forms of wildlife around their home in the Pacific Northwest.